```
J                    566273
920                   18.60
Bou
Bourne
The Big golden book of
Christopher Columbus and
other early adventurers
```

DATE DUE			

GREAT RIVER REGIONAL LIBRARY

St. Cloud, Minnesota 56301

S0-EWY-925

Christopher Columbus

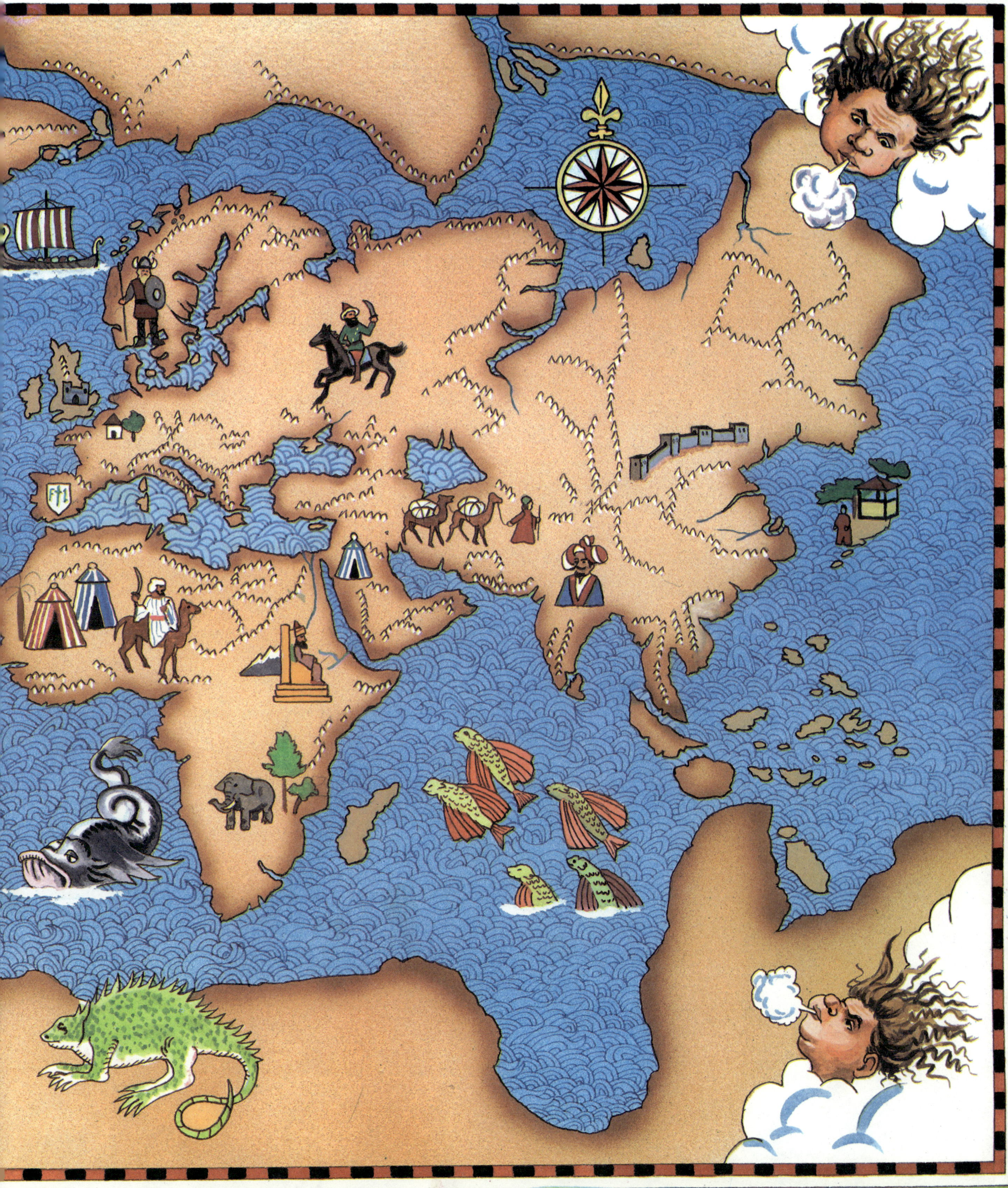

A GOLDEN BOOK • NEW YORK
Western Publishing Company, Inc., Racine, Wisconsin 53404

© 1991 Russell Bourne. Illustrations © 1991 Thomas LaPadula. All rights reserved. Printed in the U.S.A. No part of this book may be reproduced or copied in any form without written permission from the publisher. All trademarks are the property of Western Publishing Company, Inc. Library of Congress Catalog Card Number: 90-84253. ISBN: 0-307-17870-6/ISBN: 0-307-67870-9 (lib. bdg.)   A MCMXCI

THE BIG GOLDEN BOOK OF
CHRISTOPHER COLUMBUS
and Other Early Adventurers

By Russell Bourne
Illustrated by Thomas LaPadula

To Mickey and Molly

Introduction

About five hundred years ago, in 1492, three ships raised their sails in the harbor of Palos, a town on the Atlantic coast of Spain. The tide was going out, filling the air with the smell of salt and fish, seaweed and rotting wood. The day was clear and sea gulls swept across the sky, filling the air with their harsh cries.

Slowly the ships eased from the harbor mouth. Breaking out more sail, they headed west. Before them lay the Atlantic Ocean, a stretch of storm-tossed sea so broad that no living person had ever seen its end.

A man named Christopher Columbus commanded all three ships. He was an Italian serving the king and queen of Spain. And although he set out looking for something else, Columbus was about to become famous as the man who discovered America.

INDIANS AND VIKINGS

We now know that Columbus was not the first person to discover America. For one thing, people were already living there when he arrived. Today we call these people Native Americans. You also know them by another name, the name that Columbus gave them: Indians.

Columbus wasn't even the first European to find America. Four or five hundred years earlier, people from northern Europe called Vikings had visited and settled there.

But we still think of Columbus as the discoverer of America, and for good reason. The Vikings left no history of their voyage, and only recently were historians able to prove that they had visited at all. The Viking settlements did not last. And for the next four or five hundred years, no other European saw America.

The year 1492 was the start of an amazing one hundred years of exploration. At that time, Europeans knew almost nothing about the world. But after Columbus returned to Spain, news of his voyage spread all over Europe. By 1592 Europeans were living in America and Africa. They were voyaging far to the east to trade with the empires of Asia. And European ships had twice sailed around the world, a voyage of more than twenty-five thousand miles.

No one-hundred-year period of exploration was more remarkable—unless it turns out to be the present one that started in 1961, when a Russian named Yuri Gagarin became the first person to fly into space.

CHANGING THE WORLD

What made Europeans so eager to explore the world? Some went for adventure, to test their courage and skill and to see new and wonderful things. Some went to escape troubles and start a new life. Some wanted riches and glory—and stopped at nothing to get them. And some went to spread Christianity to new lands.

Whatever their reasons, they changed the world. In that hundred years the known world ceased to be a small place, bound by uncrossable oceans. It had grown to be as big as their imaginations. New worlds and new ideas were waiting to be explored by anyone brave enough to try. A new feeling of possibility sent them around the world, just as it is now sending us into space.

The Weaver's Son

The boy's name was Christoforo Colombo, and he was in love with the sea. He loved the sound the waves made against the pebbled shore and the smell and taste of the sea wind. The broad blue horizon of the sea seemed to call out to him.

Christoforo—whom we call Christopher Columbus—was the son of a weaver, a maker of cloth. He lived in a seaport city called Genoa in Italy. Christopher spent most of each day helping his father, as many children did then. But the red-haired boy, with blue eyes and lanky body, went down to the docks whenever he could. He went to hear the tales the sailors told and the music of sails snapping and crackling in the wind. He went to watch the ships slip away like dreams to faraway places.

THE YOUNG SAILOR

Christopher's father bought wool for weaving from many places, and his cloth went by ship to distant cities. So when Christopher was old enough, he began to sail with the wool and cloth along the coasts of Italy, France, and Spain. On these voyages he learned as much as he could. How far did the sea extend? Who had sailed to its end?

SEA MONSTERS AND MERMAIDS

Where people's knowledge ended, their imaginations began. They talked of sea monsters and giants, mermaids and terrible creatures of every kind. Some said that the world was flat, not round, and that to sail too far was to risk falling off its edge.

But Christopher wanted to *know*, not to imagine. He felt that it must be possible to find out the truth. His parents had named him for Saint Christopher, who was believed to have once crossed a river carrying Christ on his back. In his daydreams, Chistopher Columbus wondered if he, too, was meant to cross the water, carrying the message of Christ to distant lands.

There wasn't much to be known. Some people believed that the world was round, because an ancient Greek had used mathematics to demonstrate it. But no one knew for sure. The best maps of the time showed Europe and the lands around the Mediterranean Sea, which washes Europe's southern shores. Few people had ever traveled farther. The most famous of these were Marco Polo and his family, who reached China in 1275, nearly two hundred years before Christopher was born.

About Marco Polo and the Empire of Cathay

Marco Polo was only seventeen when he left his home in Venice, Italy, with his father and uncle. They were traders who had found a way to a country no European had ever seen. They called it Cathay but today we call it China.

They reached China in 1275 after a hard and dangerous journey that brought them a third of the way around the world and lasted two years. The emperor of China, Kublai Khan, took a liking to Marco and his family. They stayed in China for the next seventeen years, serving the emperor. Marco traveled throughout China. He saw the wonders of this exotic land: beautiful silks, brilliant jewels, huge cities, mighty rivers—even rockets and paper money.

Finally Marco and his family left for home, reaching Venice twenty-four years after they had left. Marco told his story to a writer named Rustichello, who, sometime around the year 1300, wrote a book about Marco's travels. It was to feed the dreams of other explorers, including Columbus, for centuries to come.

Battle at Sea

The older Christopher grew, the more time he spent at sea. Now he was no longer just riding along with his father's goods. He was a paid seaman helping to sail the ship. And he soon learned that the sea offered danger as well as beauty and adventure.

Christopher was in his early twenties when he got a job on a ship sailing from Genoa to England. They were not long at sea when they were attacked by ships from France. In the terrible and bloody battle, Christopher was first wounded and then thrown into the sea as his ship went to the bottom of the ocean. By luck, he found an oar. Clinging to it, he began to swim. He swam and rested, swam and rested for six miles. Finally, hurt and exhausted, he washed up on the coast of Portugal.

Again, luck was with him. Many people from his home city of Genoa lived in Lisbon, Portugal's chief city. They took him in and cared for him until he was strong. Then they urged him to stay, because Lisbon had become Europe's center for exploration.

It was a hard decision for Christopher. It meant turning his back on home and family and starting a new life. But after much thought, he decided to stay. It proved to be one of the most important decisions he ever made.

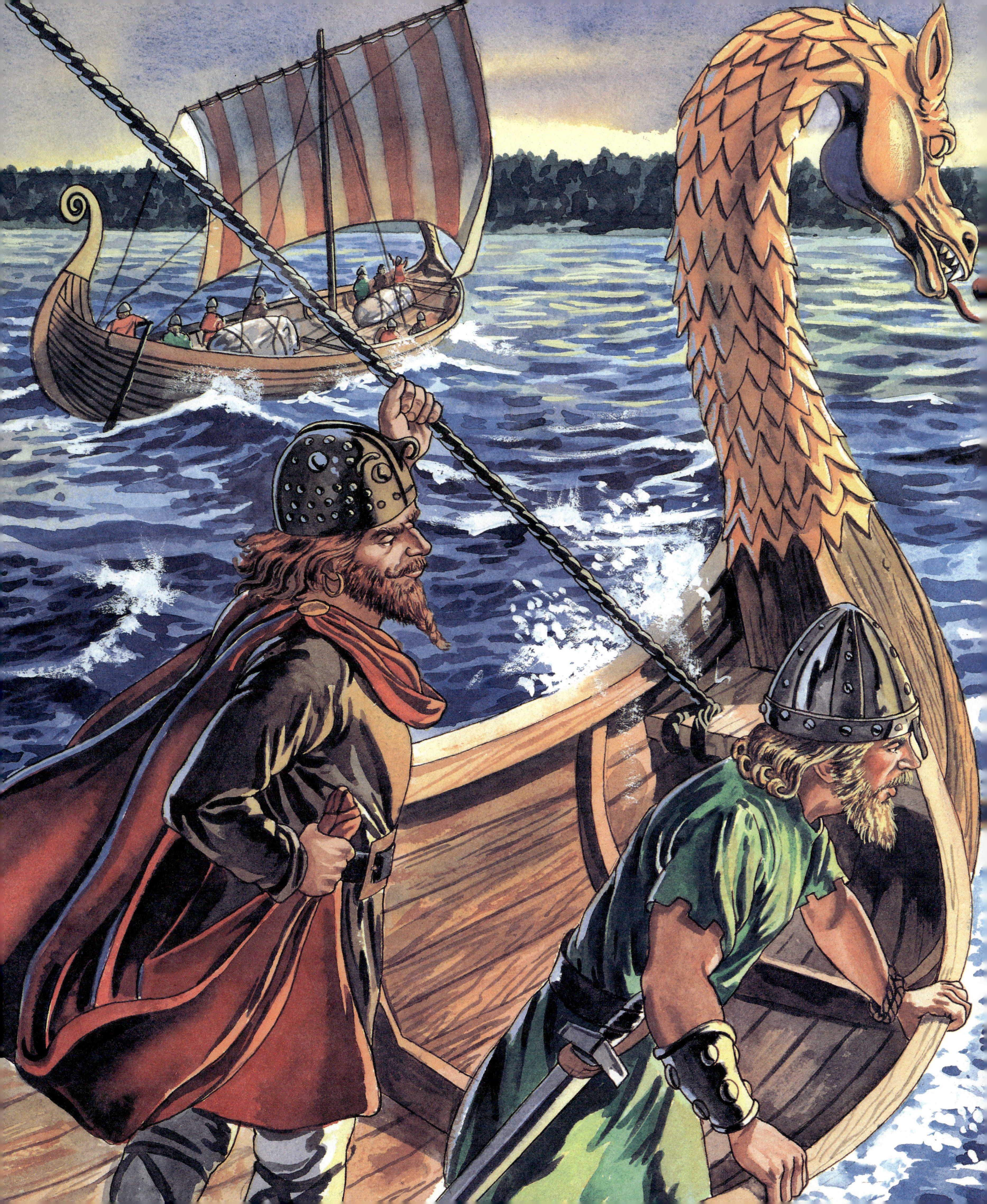

Home of the Vikings

Christopher had not gone to school as a boy. In Portugal, however, he learned not only to speak Portuguese but to read and write it as well. He also learned Spanish, the language of Spain, Portugal's neighbor. It was hard work learning so much, but Christopher had a deep hunger for knowledge. He never seemed to get enough.

He also continued the work he loved: sailing ships. In 1477 he sailed to England and Ireland, and then on to a rocky island far to the north called Iceland. This island is closer to America than any other part of Europe. Columbus may have heard stories in Iceland about the voyages of the Vikings far into the western seas.

STORIES FROM VINLAND

In the language of Iceland, Viking is a word that means exploring. Stories told how the Vikings had found a beautiful land far to the west. They called it Vinland, or "wine land," because of the grapes that grew there. The Vikings made a home in Vinland, so the stories went, and fought bloody battles with the natives. Then nothing more was ever heard from them.

Were the stories true? For hundreds of years no one knew. Certainly the Vikings were brave and skillful sailors, and they had strong and beautiful ships that could have made the trip. But scientists have only recently found the homes that the Vikings built on what today we call Newfoundland, the easternmost part of Canada. So the Vikings did reach North America soon after the year 1000 and founded the first European settlement there. But, we believe, battling the natives and the terrible winters was too much for them, and the colony died out.

A Dream Is Born

Christopher Columbus is famous because he dreamed a great dream and had the courage and skill to act on it. Maybe the dream took hold of him in Iceland as he listened to the stories. Maybe it began to form before he ever set foot on a ship. He was not the first person to think of this idea, but he was the first to bet his life on it.

The dream was to reach Asia by sailing *west* rather than east. It was a dream that Europeans would follow for centuries after Columbus raised sail.

Why did Europeans want to reach Asia? There were two reasons: silk and spices. Silk is a beautiful, soft, shiny cloth. Spices make food last longer and taste better. But all silk and many spices, including pepper, came only from Asia at that time. Rich people in Europe were willing to pay huge prices for such things. Sometimes they paid as much for pepper—the same pepper that sits on your table—as they did for gold!

The Triumph of Bartholomeu Dias

In 1487 Portugal's King John II sent Bartholomeu Dias to sail south down the coast of Africa. He was looking for a way to turn east toward Asia. Other explorers had tried, but Africa is a vast land and they had never come to its end.

Dias sailed farther than anyone else and finally rounded the southern tip of Africa into the Indian Ocean, which no European since Marco Polo had seen. The Portuguese called Africa's southern tip the Cape of Good Hope, because it had opened a new way for Portugal to reach the riches of the Indies, as Europeans called Asia then.

Columbus was at King John's court on the day in 1488 when Dias returned. He heard Dias speak of strange birds (flamingos and penguins) he had seen, and of the great storms and freezing waters he had faced. Christopher also saw the honors and rich gifts the king gave Dias, a battered but noble hero.

And so another piece was added to Christopher's dream. Waiting for him to the west was more than adventure, more than a chance to learn and a chance to teach the Christian faith—wealth and glory were waiting there as well.

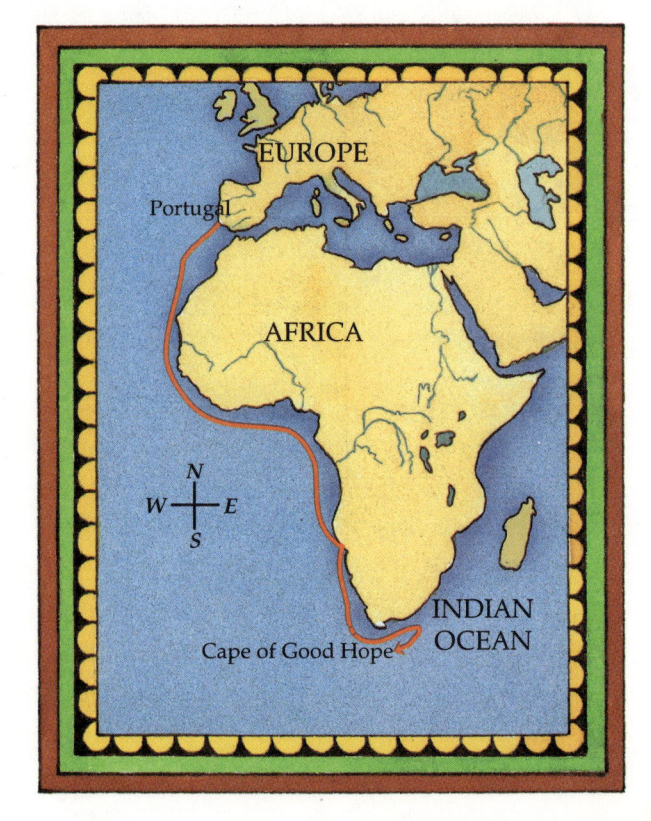

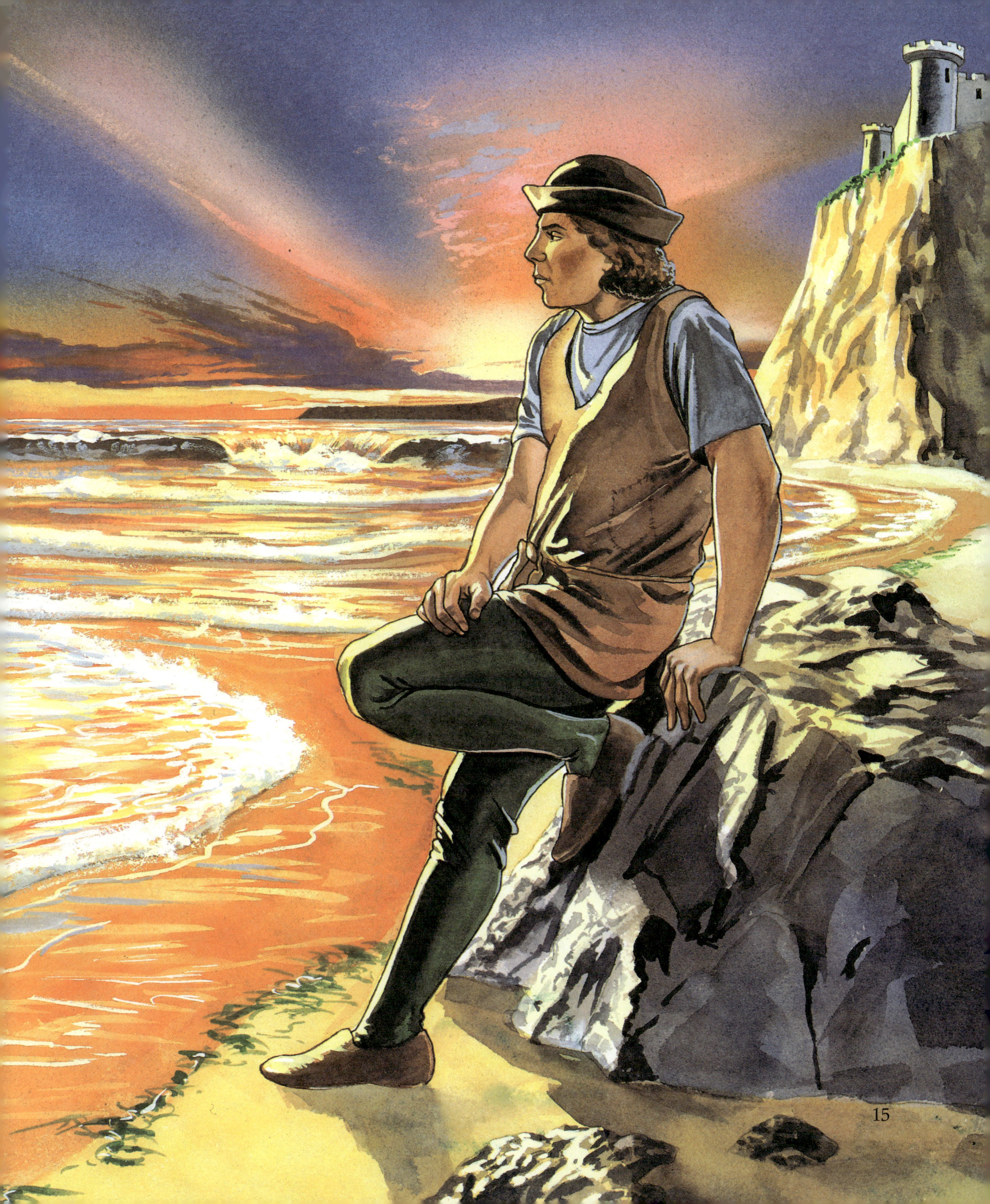

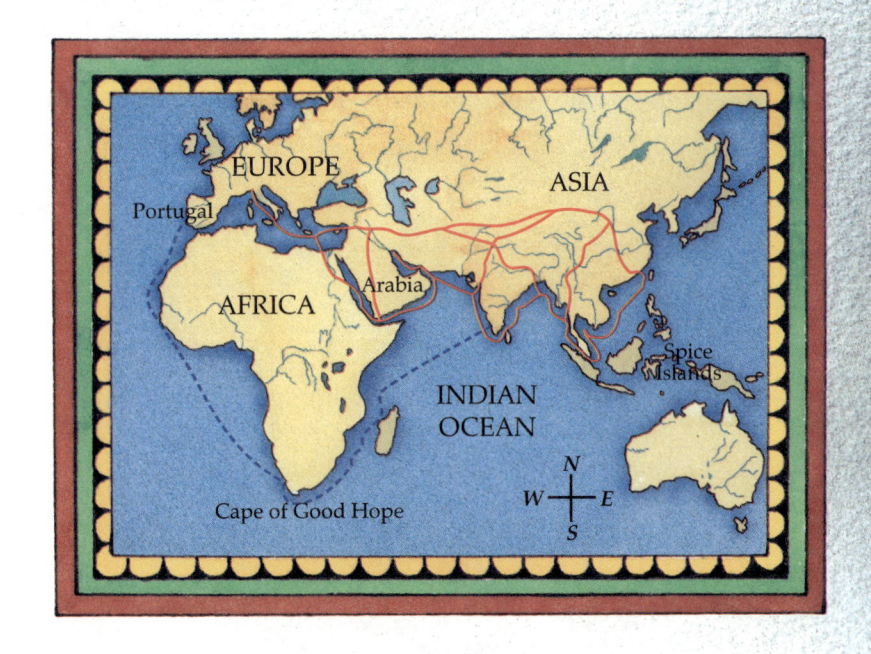

The Spice Routes

Because people would pay for silk and spices, traders would do almost anything to get them. Asia lay to the east of Europe, so they went east by land. After Dias, they sailed around the Cape of Good Hope. Either way, it was a dangerous journey.

Columbus was not alone in wondering if the Indies could be reached by sailing west. If the world was round, it didn't matter which way you went. But how far was it if you sailed west? No one knew. Columbus listened carefully to every story about islands to the west. He read books containing guesses about how large the world might be! He learned as much as he could about navigating a ship from one place to another.

Help From the King and Queen

It took much more money than Columbus had to buy ships, hire a crew, and stock the food and other things he needed for a long voyage. So he asked the king and queen of Portugal to pay for everything. If he could truly find a faster and easier route to Asia, it would make Portugal one of the richest nations on Earth.

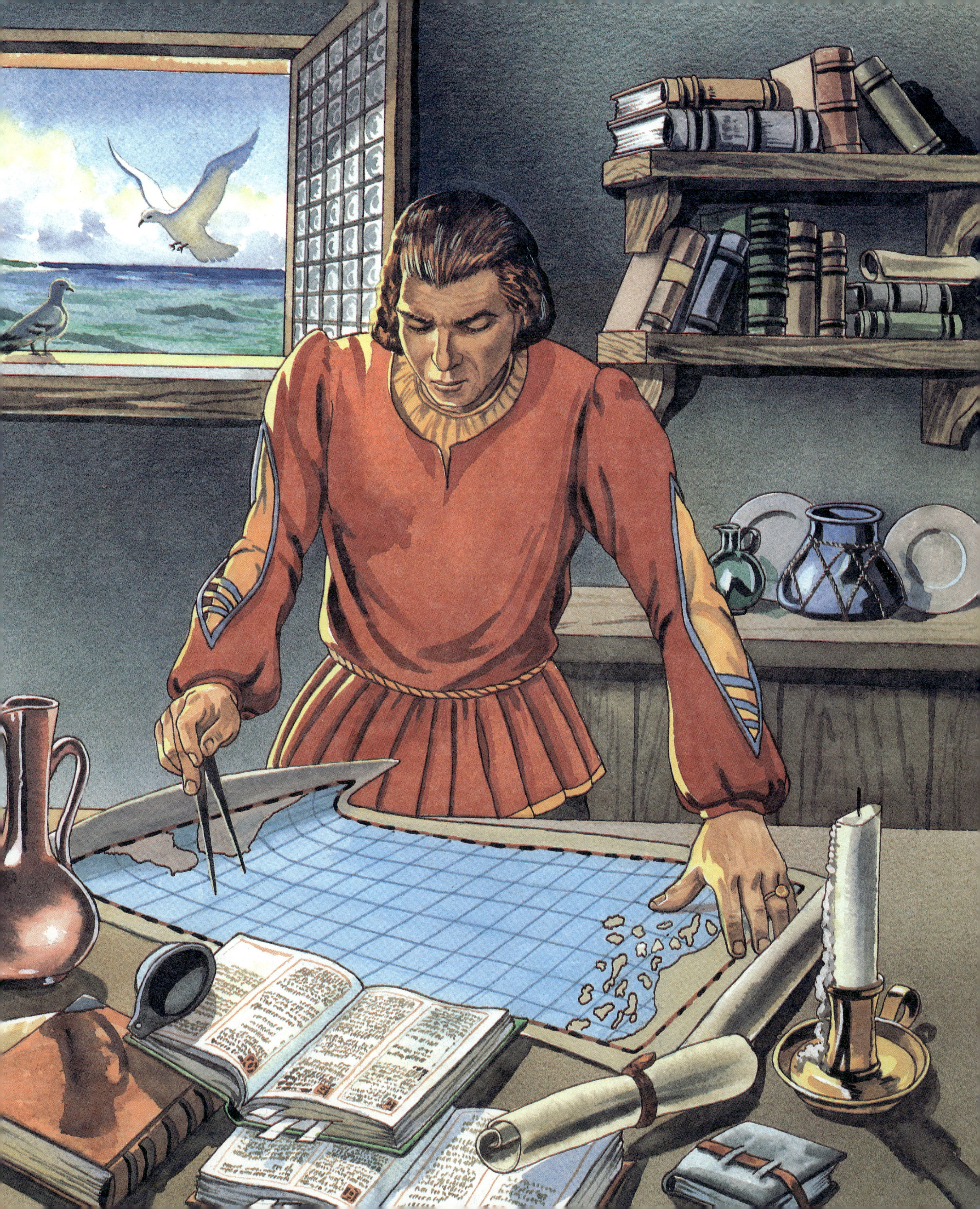

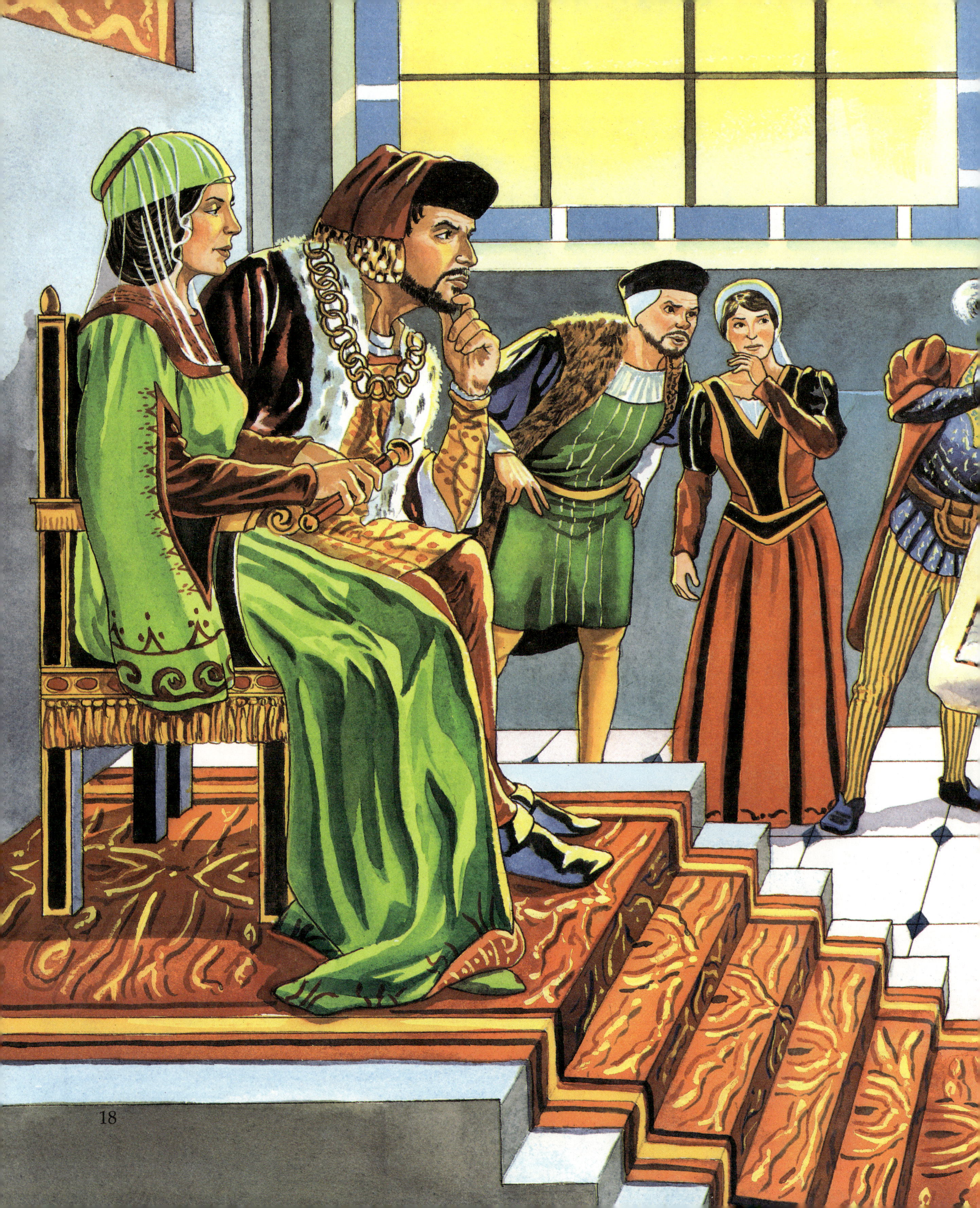

The Enterprise of the Indies

Columbus faced a big challenge in 1484 when he presented his ideas to the king and queen of Portugal. He was asking them to risk a lot of money on a dream. The only thing Columbus was risking was his life—important to him, of course, but not necessarily to the king and queen.

He called his idea the Enterprise of the Indies. He told the king and queen that he could reach the Indies by sailing west only three thousand five hundred miles, a manageable distance by sea. If they would give him three ships, he promised to open a new way west and to claim all lands he found on the way for Portugal. In return, he demanded more rewards and honors, perhaps, than an untested explorer should expect.

A ROYAL NO

After listening carefully, the king and queen turned him down. They had already spent a great deal of money on trying to open the eastern route that Bartholomeu Dias championed. They also listened to learned men who told them Columbus was completely wrong about how far away the Indies were. As it turned out, these men made a better guess than Christopher did: The actual distance westward by sea from Portugal to Asia is closer to sixteen thousand miles, more than four times farther than Columbus thought.

Isabella the Queen

Christopher did not give up. Next he turned to France, England, and finally, in 1486, Spain. At the court of King Ferdinand and Queen Isabella on the first of May, he once again described his ideas and asked for royal help. At first everything seemed to go well. The queen, as redheaded as Columbus, seemed to like him and to be excited by the voyage he described. She put Columbus in touch with the king's treasurer, Luis de Santangel—which gave Columbus hope.

But for six years nothing happened. Columbus sold books and maps to support himself while he waited. Then, early in 1492, the king and queen said no.

Deeply disappointed, Columbus packed his belongings on a mule and left the Spanish capital. But as he trudged along a mountain road, horsemen from the court caught up with him. To his amazement, they told him that the queen had changed her mind. Luis de Santangel had promised to raise most of the money himself. Now Isabella was willing to borrow the rest against the value of her jewels.

ADMIRAL OF THE OCEAN SEA

The king and queen agreed to everything Columbus wanted. Named Admiral of the Ocean Sea, he was also given three ships.

The *Niña* and *Pinta* were caravels, a new kind of ship with a European hull and the sort of sails used by the Arab ships of the Mediterranean. Caravels were strong enough to cross the ocean but small and light enough to explore shallow waters. Each carried twenty-five sailors. The third ship, the *Santa María*, was bigger and heavier and had a crew of forty. Columbus began the voyage on the *Santa María*, but the *Pinta*—his favorite—became his flagship.

On August 3, 1492, the Admiral of the Ocean Sea, now more than forty years old, ordered his ships to raise anchor from the seaport of Palos. As the sun set that day, they had left land far behind. As far as the eye could see lay the ocean, painted with the colors of blood and fire by the setting sun.

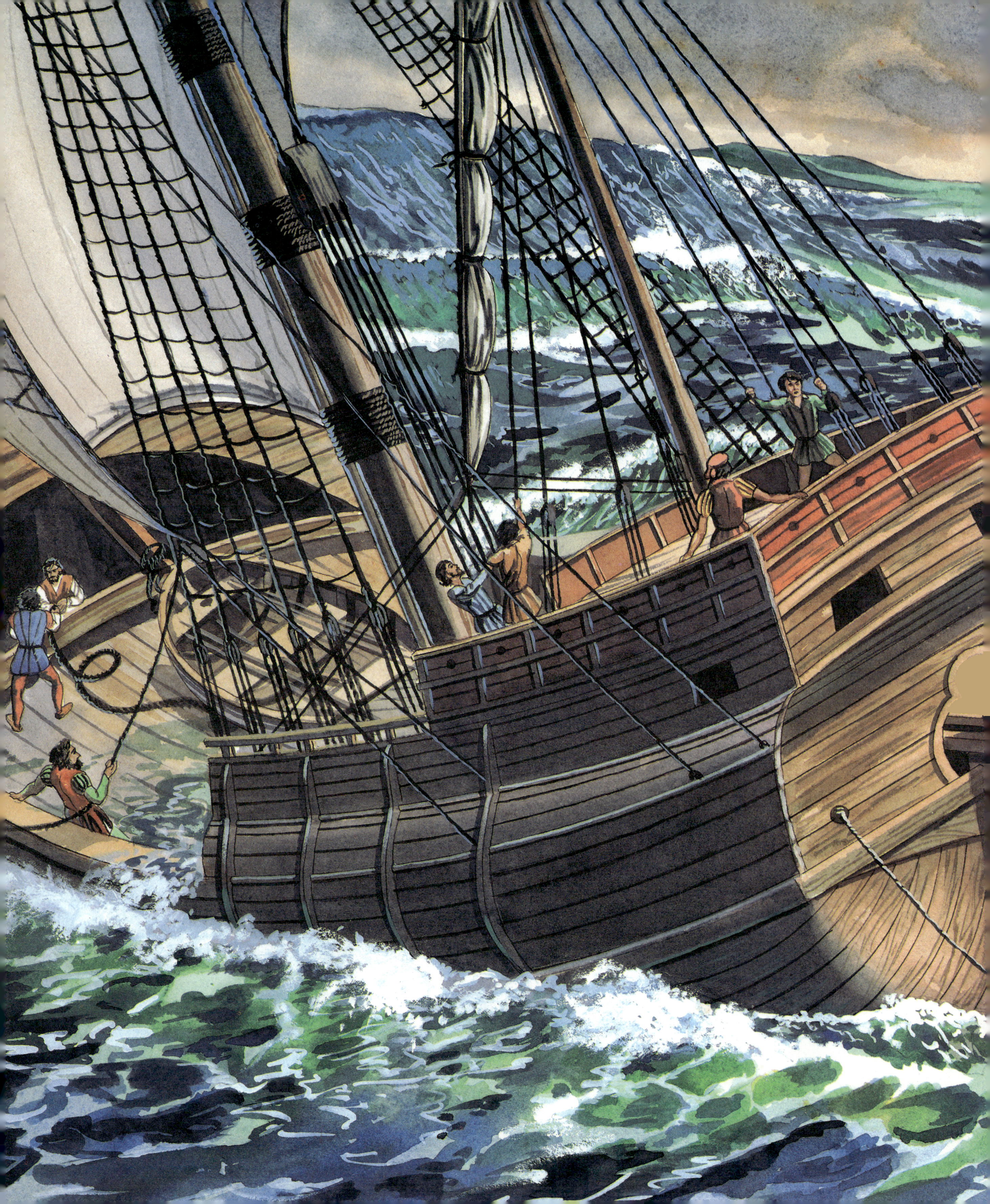

Hard Days at Sea

"How great a pleasure is the taste of the mornings!" Christopher Columbus wrote in the journal he kept. After eight years of dreams, hopes, and disappointments, he was very happy. No matter what dangers arose, the Enterprise of the Indies was on its way.

Life aboard the *Santa María* soon fell into the rhythms of a ship at sea. Someone must always steer the vessel and control the sails. When the sailors were not taking turns at these jobs, they slept, played games, or mended clothes. And they spent as much time as they could on deck.

To our eyes, Columbus's ships would have looked terrifyingly small. The men lived in a dark, evil-smelling room seventy or eighty feet long, twelve feet wide, and with a ceiling about six feet high—a room about twice the size of a motor home. Now imagine forty men (who never bathed), barrels of food and drink, and heaps of sails and other supplies all squeezed into that space. There were no fresh fruits or vegetables, only salted meat and hard bread. Most of the sailors slept on bunks so tightly stacked that the men could not sit up in bed. No wonder the sailors liked to stay on deck!

TWO LOGBOOKS

The sailors were led by the ship's officers and, on the *Santa María*, the admiral. Among their jobs was navigation, keeping track of where the ship was. But as the ships sailed farther and farther west, Columbus took over all navigation.

He had his reasons. By doing all the work himself, he could keep two logbooks. His own secret book gave the true distance. A second book, open for all to see, made the distance seem much shorter. Columbus knew that they had sailed too far to turn back—they would run out of food and water before reaching Spain.

24

Land! Land!

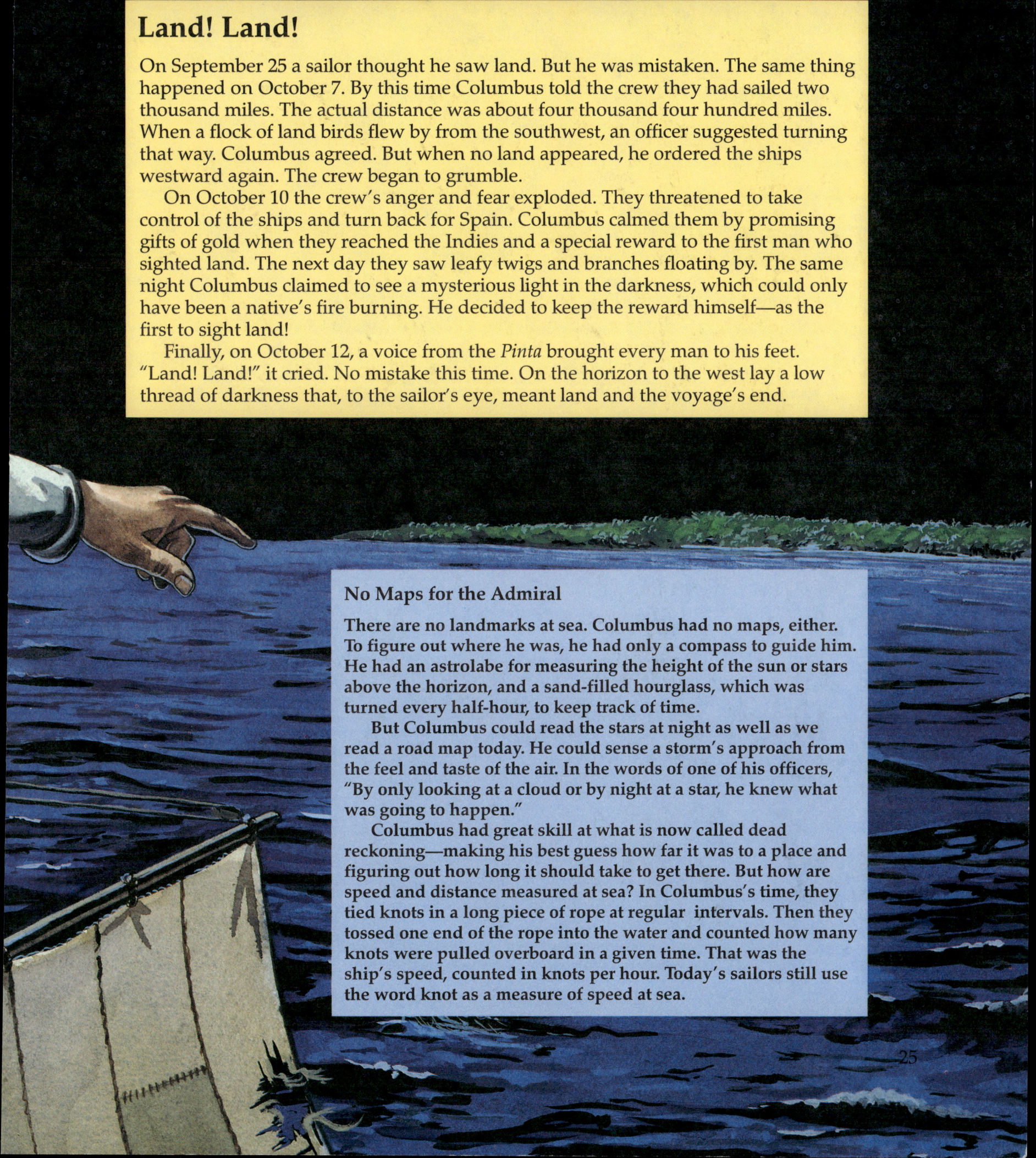

On September 25 a sailor thought he saw land. But he was mistaken. The same thing happened on October 7. By this time Columbus told the crew they had sailed two thousand miles. The actual distance was about four thousand four hundred miles. When a flock of land birds flew by from the southwest, an officer suggested turning that way. Columbus agreed. But when no land appeared, he ordered the ships westward again. The crew began to grumble.

On October 10 the crew's anger and fear exploded. They threatened to take control of the ships and turn back for Spain. Columbus calmed them by promising gifts of gold when they reached the Indies and a special reward to the first man who sighted land. The next day they saw leafy twigs and branches floating by. The same night Columbus claimed to see a mysterious light in the darkness, which could only have been a native's fire burning. He decided to keep the reward himself—as the first to sight land!

Finally, on October 12, a voice from the *Pinta* brought every man to his feet. "Land! Land!" it cried. No mistake this time. On the horizon to the west lay a low thread of darkness that, to the sailor's eye, meant land and the voyage's end.

No Maps for the Admiral

There are no landmarks at sea. Columbus had no maps, either. To figure out where he was, he had only a compass to guide him. He had an astrolabe for measuring the height of the sun or stars above the horizon, and a sand-filled hourglass, which was turned every half-hour, to keep track of time.

But Columbus could read the stars at night as well as we read a road map today. He could sense a storm's approach from the feel and taste of the air. In the words of one of his officers, "By only looking at a cloud or by night at a star, he knew what was going to happen."

Columbus had great skill at what is now called dead reckoning—making his best guess how far it was to a place and figuring out how long it should take to get there. But how are speed and distance measured at sea? In Columbus's time, they tied knots in a long piece of rope at regular intervals. Then they tossed one end of the rope into the water and counted how many knots were pulled overboard in a given time. That was the ship's speed, counted in knots per hour. Today's sailors still use the word knot as a measure of speed at sea.

Landfall in the Bahamas

In a fine display of seamanship, Columbus had crossed some four thousand miles of ocean in only seventy days. He was still more than twelve thousand four hundred miles short of Asia, but he had no way of knowing it.

He had found one of the many beautiful islands that all together are called the Bahamas. They are about four hundred miles east of Florida.

SAN SALVADOR

Historians today disagree over whether the island Columbus found was Watlings Island or Samana Cay. In either case, he was lucky to have sighted it. A tiny spot in the vastness of the ocean, the island was only six miles wide and thirteen miles long. If he had not turned his ships southwest a few days before, he would have missed this island and possibly all the others. He would then have entered the Gulf Stream, an ocean current flowing north and east, and might have been swept out of sight of land.

Columbus found a safe place to drop anchor and then led a group of sailors and officers ashore. After so many days at sea, it was good to stand on dry land again, to smell its rich smells and hear the calling of birds. With the king's banner in his hand, he stood on top of a green hill and claimed the island for King Ferdinand and Queen Isabella of Spain. Full of pride, he named it San Salvador, which means Holy Savior.

27

People From the Sky

Columbus and his men soon found that they were not alone on the island. Handsome dark-skinned people came to greet the explorers. Columbus noticed the bits of gold they wore in their ears and noses. Here was the promise of the huge treasure he needed to repay the king and queen. He was even more excited when the natives told him, in sign language, that he would find more gold on islands farther south and west.

The natives were Arawaks, a simple, peaceful group of Native Americans. But Columbus called them Indians, the people of the Indies. These people did not have the silks or spices or gleaming temples that Marco Polo had described. But Columbus was not worried. He believed that he had not yet reached Asia itself—only one of the thousands of islands that Marco Polo had said lay near its coast.

To the Arawaks, the explorers were "People from the Sky." With their white skins, strange clothes, and great ships, they seemed like gods, and the Arawaks were eager to help. Columbus thought they could easily be turned into Christians. Perhaps he could now fulfill his lifelong dream of bearing Christ's message across the deep water.

Columbus also thought that the Arawaks could be trained as servants. And in this belief he was sadly right. In return for the Arawaks' help, the Spanish would enslave them and would finally wipe them off the face of the Earth.

After resting and taking on fresh food and water, Columbus set sail again. He took a few Arawaks as guides to help him find a larger island nearby, which they called Coiba. We call it Cuba today. Columbus was sure, however, that it must be Cipangu, which we call Japan, a land of great riches.

Search for Cipangu

The island of Cuba rose slowly over the horizon as Columbus's ships drew near. The air shimmered with heat, and thick green forests rose from the shore to the peaks of rugged mountains. Here, too, the natives who greeted them wore small pieces of gold jewelry. They also had a strange habit of setting fire to bits of a dried weed and breathing the smoke. Today that weed is known around the world as tobacco. But the island itself was nothing like Cipangu or Cathay, as Marco Polo had described them.

Disappointed, Columbus sailed on until he came to another island, which he named Hispaniola. On today's maps, the nations of Haiti and the Dominican Republic share this island. To Columbus, Hispaniola was the most beautiful and promising of all the islands he had seen. The natives here seemed to have more gold, which they found among the pebbles on the bottoms of streams. Columbus thought that more could be dug from the ground, enough to please the king and queen.

But in reaching Hispaniola, Columbus lost the largest of his three ships when the *Santa María* ran aground and was wrecked. The admiral decided to return to Spain at once before something happened to the remaining ships. But his whole crew could not fit aboard the *Niña* and *Pinta*. Columbus decided to put forty men ashore to search for gold and to build a town, which Columbus named Navidad. He hoped that by the time he returned, he would find buildings put up and a rich gold mine started as well.

A HERO'S WELCOME

Columbus's arrival in Spain was everything he could have hoped for. He had proved that the Indies could be reached by sailing west—or so he thought—and that the distance was not much greater than he had claimed. He was a hero, and huge crowds came to see his Arawak captives, colorful parrots, and other curiosities. The pieces of gold he brought to the king and queen seemed to hold the promise of great riches to come. Ferdinand and Isabella were greatly pleased. They invited Columbus to sit beside them and to keep his hat on in their presence. It was a remarkable sign of royal pleasure.

The Fate of Navidad

All the wealth of the Indies appeared to be waiting, needing only men to find it and carry it home. In short order, the king and queen sent out another expedition. This time, Columbus led a fleet of seventeen ships carrying more than one thousand two hundred men. Their job was to found a colony on Hispaniola and start sending gold to Spain. Ferdinand and Isabella named Columbus governor of the colony and promised him a rich share of the treasure. He, in turn, invited his brother Diego to go with him.

On this voyage of 1493, Columbus steered farther to the south, in hopes of finding the mainland of the Indies. Instead, he came to the Caribbean Sea, and his ships explored the islands they found there. Finally Christopher led the way back to Hispaniola—where a frightening shock awaited them.

THE ARAWAKS REBEL

The men left behind at Navidad found the work of searching for gold too hard. So they settled for stealing the Arawaks' gold, along with food and anything else they felt like taking. Eventually, the enraged Arawaks killed the Spaniards.

Shocked by the massacre, Columbus grieved for the lives lost, but he never thought of giving up. He founded a second colony, naming it Isabella for the queen. With more than a thousand Spaniards guarding the new town, he feared no further attack. He placed his brother Diego in command and, putting Hispaniola out of his mind, sailed off again with several ships. He was determined to find the Indies once and for all.

Columbus sailed first to Cuba where he explored its long coast, now sure that it was part of the mainland of the Indies. After reaching its westernmost coast, he decided that this body of land was so large that it *must* be Asia. He also explored the island of Jamaica, where strange plants grew: pineapples, sweet potatoes, and other fruits and vegetables that no European had ever tasted. But there was no gold.

THE WAY OF THE WARRIOR

Returning to Hispaniola, Columbus found the grim story of Navidad being repeated. The Spanish had been so cruel to the natives that war had broken out. To make matters worse, half of the colonists called for a new governor. Messages had already gone to Spain, complaining that neither Columbus nor his brother knew how to rule.

Columbus faced a painful choice. He could try to make peace with the Arawaks. It would fulfill his dream of carrying Christ's message to distant shores. But the only way to make peace was to start treating the Arawaks justly.

But would the Spaniards obey? And what could he do if they refused? The colony would turn against him, and his other dreams—the new voyages he planned, the wealth and glory he thought he deserved—would be destroyed.

Buckling on sword and armor, Columbus chose the warrior's way. He led the Spaniards in an attack that wiped out the Arawaks—men, women, and children. The few who survived became slaves of the Spanish conquerors.

When news of the slaughter reached Ferdinand and Isabella, this seemed yet another sign that Columbus could not rule the colony. In 1496 they sent an inspector to Hispaniola to learn the truth. But on his arrival, Columbus hurriedly set sail for Spain. Whatever the inspector might report, the Admiral wanted to reach the king and queen first with his own story—and with more gold.

Discovery and Defeat

Once again, the king and queen listened as their admiral told them of his travels. The small amount of gold that Columbus brought was disappointing. And they were sorry that their new lands were held by the sword rather than by the cross.

But they still had confidence in Columbus. Whatever his failings, he had found vast new lands to the west. And there was still the promise of wealth there, for where there was a little gold, there might be much more.

In May of 1498 Columbus sailed yet again, at the head of a small fleet of six ships. He set a course still farther south than before and came at last to a great green coast running north and south as far as the eye could see. Broad rivers poured their waters into the sea, rivers so large that Columbus wrote: "I believe that this is a very great continent, which until today has been unknown."

Columbus had actually discovered South America. But he was wondering what part of Asia it might be. The question haunted him. Where were the fabled empires of Cipangu and Cathay? They always seemed to lay just beyond the horizon.

THE ADMIRAL IN CHAINS

By August, Columbus once again reached Hispaniola and again he took charge. But he was, in fact, as poor a governor as the colonists said. At sea he was a strong leader, but on land his powers of leadership always seemed to desert him. Soon a royal commissioner arrived from Spain to take charge in the king's name. He went so far as to seize Columbus's own gold and other property. He also charged Columbus with crimes and had the explorer bound in chains and sent to Spain for trial.

It was a dark and humiliating voyage for Christopher Columbus. But even humiliation has its uses. The captain of the ship began to feel sorry for Columbus. He offered to take off the heavy chains. But Columbus refused. He hoped that if the king and queen saw him like this, it would mean more than any words could say.

The High Voyage

Columbus was right. Ferdinand and Isabella were horrified by the chains. They ordered him released at once. By 1502 his property and titles—all except that of governor—had been returned to him, and the king and queen were willing to send him to sea again.

Columbus called this journey the "High Voyage," the adventure that would restore all his fame and fortune. He was fifty by now, and his health was beginning to fail. But he was as determined as ever. The restlessness in him, the hunger that would not be stilled, drove him west more powerfully than the ocean winds.

This time his course took him to the coast of Central America. As skilled a sailor as ever, he rode out a great storm that destroyed another Spanish fleet near Hispaniola. Then he sailed southward along the coast, still searching for Cipangu and Cathay, or for any way to turn west again. He obtained much gold by trading with the natives. And he heard stories of another great sea on the other side of the nearby mountains. Though he did not know it, Columbus was only forty miles from that mysterious ocean. He had reached Panama where, four hundred years later, a canal would link the Atlantic Ocean and the Pacific Ocean. But, unfortunately, Columbus himself never did get to the Pacific.

MAROONED

Finally he gave up and turned northward. But after a year at sea, wood-eating worms and insects had filled the ships with tiny holes. Finally, with the ships slowly sinking beneath them, Columbus ordered his men to take everything off the ships and go ashore on the island of Jamaica.

Columbus and his men were marooned for almost a year before they were rescued. He reached Spain in November of 1504 aboard a ship from Hispaniola. He had great hopes, for this time he brought with him a rich haul of gold and tales of new lands. But it was no use. His beloved Queen Isabella lay dying, and the king had no time for him. After her death, the king agreed in 1505 to hear his requests for a reward. But grief lay heavy on Ferdinand, and, without Isabella, he had little interest in Columbus.

Columbus was left with a share of the gold, which kept him comfortable if not rich. But still he could not rest. Though many doubted him, he never gave up believing that it was the Indies he had found. And he was filled with anger at the poor reward—in his eyes—that he had received. On May 20, 1506, Columbus died, proud of his victories and bitter at the ingratitude of kings.

THE FOUR VOYAGES OF COLUMBUS

- 1st Voyage
- 2nd Voyage
- 3rd Voyage
- 4th Voyage

NORTH AMERICA
CENTRAL AMERICA
Bahamas
Jamaica
Hispaniola
Panama
SOUTH AMERICA
SPAIN
AFRICA

37

Discovery of the South Sea

Like Columbus, Vasco Núñez de Balboa was a redhead. But this Spanish explorer had very different reasons for journeying into the unknown. Balboa was very good at getting into trouble, and he was usually trying not to be caught.

He went to Hispaniola in 1500 and became a farmer. But, because he owed a lot of money, he decided to move to a new colony on the coast of South America. To make his escape without paying his debts, he boarded a ship and hid, with his favorite bloodhound, in a barrel. Ordinarily, the captain would have put him ashore when he was discovered—but the expedition needed every fighting man it could find.

So—like it or not—Balboa became a soldier. In time he proved himself to be a leader. When the expedition finally reached the colony, they found it in ruins. Balboa suggested moving to nearby Panama. But, after they settled in Panama, the Spaniards arrested the governor and put Balboa in command.

Balboa began to conquer the surrounding lands, while at the same time making friends of several native chiefs. From them he heard stories of an immensely rich people called the Incas, whose land could be reached by crossing an ocean to the west.

But then Balboa heard that the colony's governor, now in Spain, had accused him of crimes. The king would soon order Balboa back to Spain to stand trial.

THE SEARCH FOR THE INCAS

If he could do something important—particularly involving gold—Balboa knew he would be safe. So he decided to lead an expedition in search of the Incas.

The search began on September 6, 1513. On September 25, standing on the top of a mountain, Balboa saw the gleam of distant water. Four days later, he reached it. Dressed in armor and with his sword held high, he splashed into the water and named it the South Sea, claiming it for Spain. Later it would be renamed the Pacific Ocean.

By the time he returned to the colony, bad news had come from Spain. Balboa escaped arrest, as he had hoped. But his bitter enemy, a man named Pedrarias, was now in charge of the colony in Panama. After several years Pedrarias arranged for someone whom Balboa thought of as a friend to accuse him of rebellion. Balboa was tried and convicted, and in January 1519 he was put to death. His faithful bloodhound, which had shared his many adventures, was poisoned by one of Balboa's enemies.

Dividing the World

By 1494 Spain and Portugal had signed a treaty dividing up the whole world. Like all conquerors, they did not care that these lands already belonged to the people living there. Spain got most of the newly discovered territory to the west (except Brazil, where people today still speak Portuguese). In addition, Portugal got Africa and India.

Portugal's problem was that the Indies were hard to reach. High mountains and broad deserts made the Indies difficult to get to by land. There were some easier land routes, but those were blocked by the Arabs. They were great traders, and most of the silks and spices that reached Europe passed through their hands. They had no wish to help the Portuguese. And there seemed no easy way to sail there, for Africa lay in the way.

THE SEARCH FOR THE INDIAN OCEAN

Unless the Portuguese could open their own route to the Indies, their half of the world would do them little good. That was why Bartholomeu Dias had been sent to sail south along the coast of Africa until he found the Cape of Good Hope and discovered where the Indian Ocean began. After that discovery, Dias hoped to be put in charge of another expedition—one meant to cross the Indian Ocean and reach India itself.

But another man was chosen to lead this expedition. No explorer, he had never sailed as far into unknown seas as Dias. But Vasco da Gama was known as a stern fighting man and a determined leader.

Da Gama Sails to India

Da Gama led four ships from Lisbon on July 8, 1497. Rather than follow the coast of Africa, as Dias had done, he steered far out into the Atlantic. His ships found the trade winds that blow steadily southeastward, and he made a swift voyage to the Cape of Good Hope. Da Gama rounded the cape in November and, landing many times to load food and water, slowly crossed the Indian Ocean. After demonstrating Portugal's firepower by bombarding Mozambique in Africa, Da Gama sailed more than two thousand miles to India. On May 22, 1498, Da Gama was hailed in the Indian city of Calicut, and warriors lined the road to honor him as he marched to the ruler's palace.

Despite this greeting, Da Gama failed in his efforts to trade with the Indians. The Arab traders did not like a European among them. Fearing that he would take part of their trade, they did everything to stop him. Finally, in August 1498, he gave up and sailed for home. Rounding the cape again, he reached Lisbon more than a year later.

Da Gama had charted a route to India that other ships would follow. Vast riches in silk and spices could be found there—if only the Arabs didn't stand in their way.

42

More Portuguese traders sailed for India and returned empty-handed. They left men behind to keep trying to trade. Then Portugal's King Manuel sent Da Gama again.

"THE VASCO DA GAMA AGE"

In 1502, Da Gama led a fleet of fourteen warships. Reaching Calicut after many months, he found that the Arabs had murdered most of the Portuguese left behind.

Da Gama's revenge was swift and sure. Europeans at that time made the best guns and most powerful cannons in the world. His warships fired on the harbor and sent most of the Arab fleet to the bottom of the sea.

After this fierce show of power, the ruler of Calicut swiftly agreed to Da Gama's terms of trade. King Manuel took great pleasure in telling the rulers of Spain that Portugal now controlled the silk and spice trade. Historians would call this "the Vasco da Gama Age," a time when Portugal controlled the wealth of all Asia.

The Mistaken Voyage

The man who made one of the greatest voyages in history did so by mistake. His ships were the first to sail all the way around the world, though he himself went only halfway. And the wrong king was paying for the trip.

MAGELLAN AND THE SPICE ISLANDS

Ferdinand Magellan was born to a noble Portuguese family about 1480. At twenty-five, he joined a fleet of merchant ships and warships sailing to India. The fleet's job was to keep Vasco Da Gama's Indian trade growing, as well as to spread Christianity. Magellan spent eight years doing both. He fought many battles, was wounded and shipwrecked, and sailed thousands of miles under the tropical sun. Hard experience made him resourceful and determined.

Magellan returned to Portugal with an idea. After establishing themselves in India, the Portuguese wished to reach a group of islands called the Moluccas, or Spice Islands. These islands were within the half of the world claimed by Portugal. But Magellan mistakenly believed that they were only a short distance from Spain's new lands. Like Columbus before him, he thought that a westward voyage would find the Spice Islands easily—if he could first discover a way around the vast lands that Columbus had claimed for Spain.

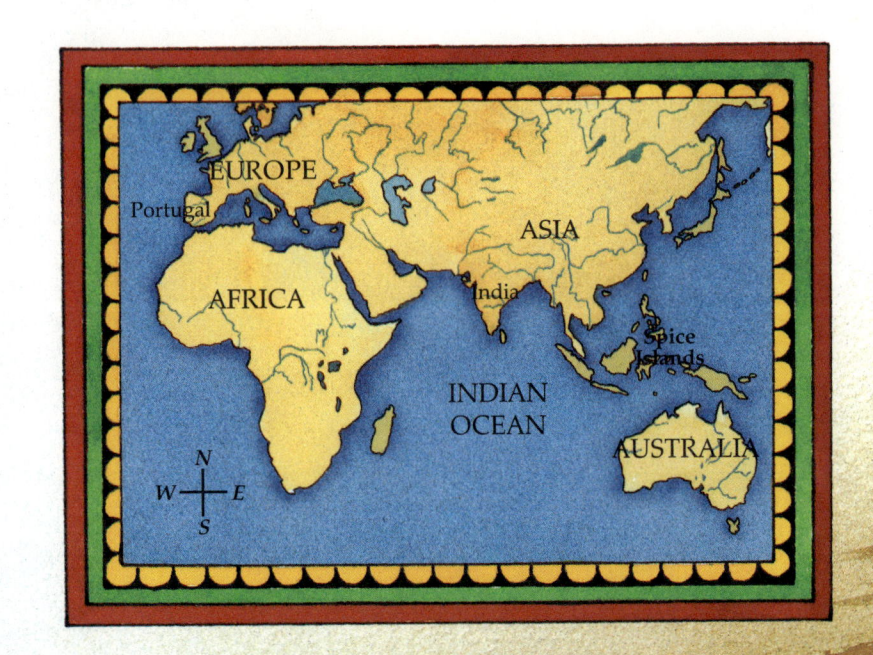

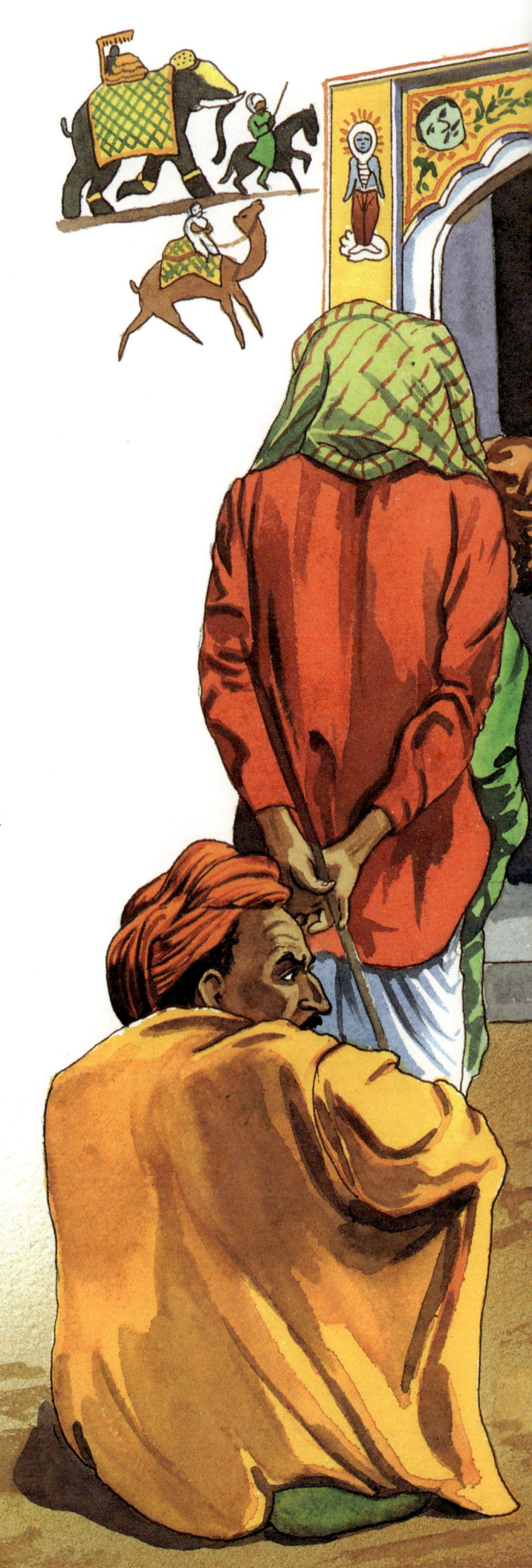

45

The Trip Around the World

Magellan's idea was not welcome in Portugal, however, because, if true, it would mean that the Spice Islands belonged to Spain. After several years there, Magellan grew discontented. He made the bold and difficult decision to offer his plan to the Spanish.

The rulers of Spain were excited by the prospect. In September of 1519 Magellan set sail from the Spanish port of Seville with five ships and about two hundred and fifty men. They sailed along South America's rocky coast, looking for a way around the continent.

It was a long, hard journey. The explorers spent a miserable winter in a camp near the tip of Argentina. Angry crewmen threatened Magellan but, with the help of loyal sailors, he defeated them. Magellan then moved his small fleet farther south, where he hoped to make a better camp. Here, in October 1520, spring in South America, a small boat found the narrow passage west that is now known as the Strait of Magellan.

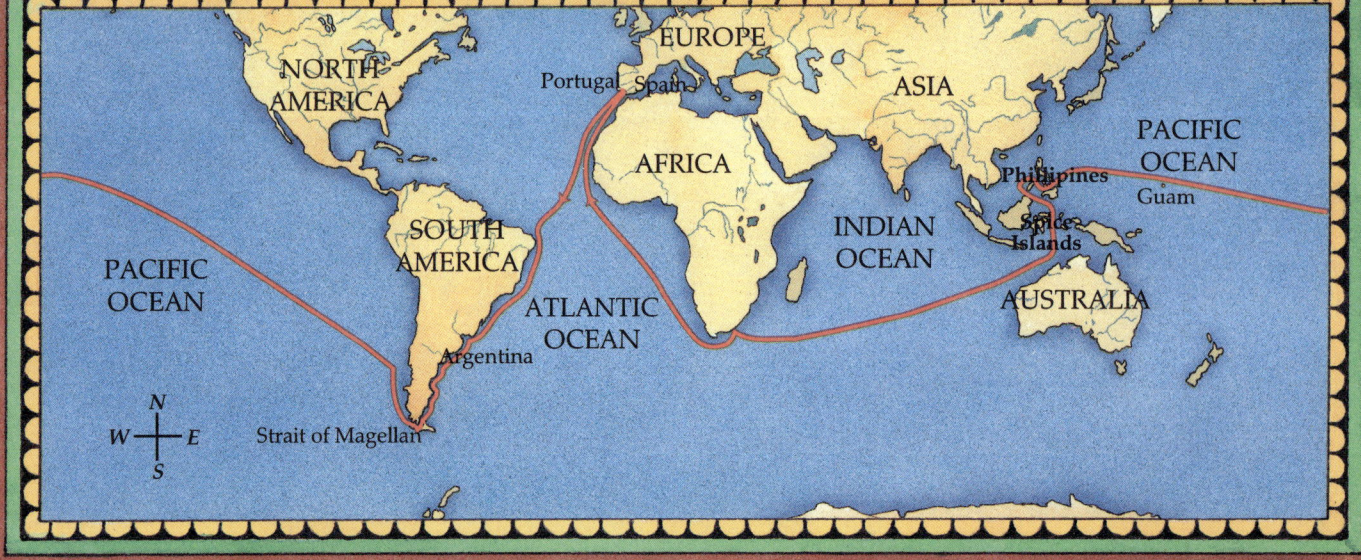

CROSSING THE PACIFIC

This narrow passage, with strong currents, huge waves, and tricky winds, is a sailor's nightmare. It took Magellan thirty-eight days to pass through it to the calmer waters of the ocean beyond. In gratitude, Magellan named this ocean Pacific, meaning "peaceful."

Shipwrecks, rebellion, and hardship left Magellan with only three ships. With no idea of the Pacific's true size, he sailed north and west into the unknown. It was nearly the death of every man aboard. For more than three months, they went without fresh food. Starvation and scurvy—a disease caused by lack of fresh fruits and vegetables—killed sailors by the dozen.

At last they reached the beautiful island of Guam and feasted on tropical fruits. Magellan then sailed another one thousand five hundred miles westward to a group of large islands now called the Philippines. Here, Magellan was determined to force the natives to become Christians—by the sword if necessary. He even joined forces with a native chief at war with another tribe. Perhaps he hoped to take over the Philippines, something the Spanish actually did forty years later. We will never know, because on April 27, 1521, the great captain was killed by the natives he had tried to conquer.

The Return of the *Victoria*

Leaderless and unsure of their mission, Magellan's men managed to do some spice trading before setting sail again. They boarded their two remaining ships, the *Victoria* and the *Trinidad*, and began the long journey home across the Indian Ocean and around Africa. The *Trinidad* had to be abandoned, and the *Victoria* limped home, sails tattered and men dying of scurvy. Of the two hundred and fifty men who began the voyage, only eighteen—the first men to sail around the world—returned to Seville.

What Day Is It?

The *Victoria* arrived in Seville on September 8, 1522. But the men aboard had kept careful count of the days and, according to them, it was September 7. What had happened?

Imagine that you live on the East Coast of the United States. At exactly twelve noon, you make a phone call to a friend on the West Coast. If you ask the time, your friend will tell you that it's nine o'clock in the morning. And your friend would be telling the truth. Here's why.

The sun rises every morning in the east. To the west—away from the sunrise—the sun rises later. For every thousand miles or so westward, the sun will rise an hour later. So the people on the West Coast see the sunrise three hours after the people on the East Coast, about three thousand miles away. If sunrise happens at five o'clock in the morning where you live, by the time the sun moves to where your friend lives, it will be eight o'clock your time and five o'clock where your friend lives.

If you keep moving west, as Magellan's men did, you keep gaining hours. Eventually, you gain twenty-four hours of time and arrive back where you started a whole day early. That's what happened to the men aboard the *Victoria*.

Today scientists have established an imaginary line—the International Date Line—in the middle of the Pacific Ocean. If you cross this line moving east, you go back to yesterday. If you cross it going west, you enter tomorrow.

U.S. West Coast 9:00

U.S. East Coast 12:00

48

A Land Called America

While the Portuguese were circumnavigating the world, Spain and other countries kept exploring the mysterious lands to the west. Were they part of the Indies? If they weren't, what wealth might they hold?

In 1523 the King of France sent an Italian explorer named Giovanni da Verrazano across the Atlantic. Verrazano explored the coast of North Carolina and traveled north looking for a passage to the Indies through the continent. He finally reported that he did not believe such a passage existed.

Twenty years earlier, another Italian named Amerigo Vespucci explored the shores of South America. Around 1500 he wrote that "it is proper to call [them] a new world." Many people called Vespucci a boaster and a liar. He claimed to have made four voyages to his "new world," while records reveal only two. He claimed that he, not Columbus, was the first man to discover South America. But whatever people thought of him, his words caught on. Today we still call the lands to the west of the Atlantic the New World.

After Vespucci's voyages, a famous mapmaker created a map of South America based on Vespucci's reports. He also suggested that the new lands be named America to honor Amerigo Vespucci. People soon began using the new name. And they came to see that North and South America were not part of Asia but entirely new lands.

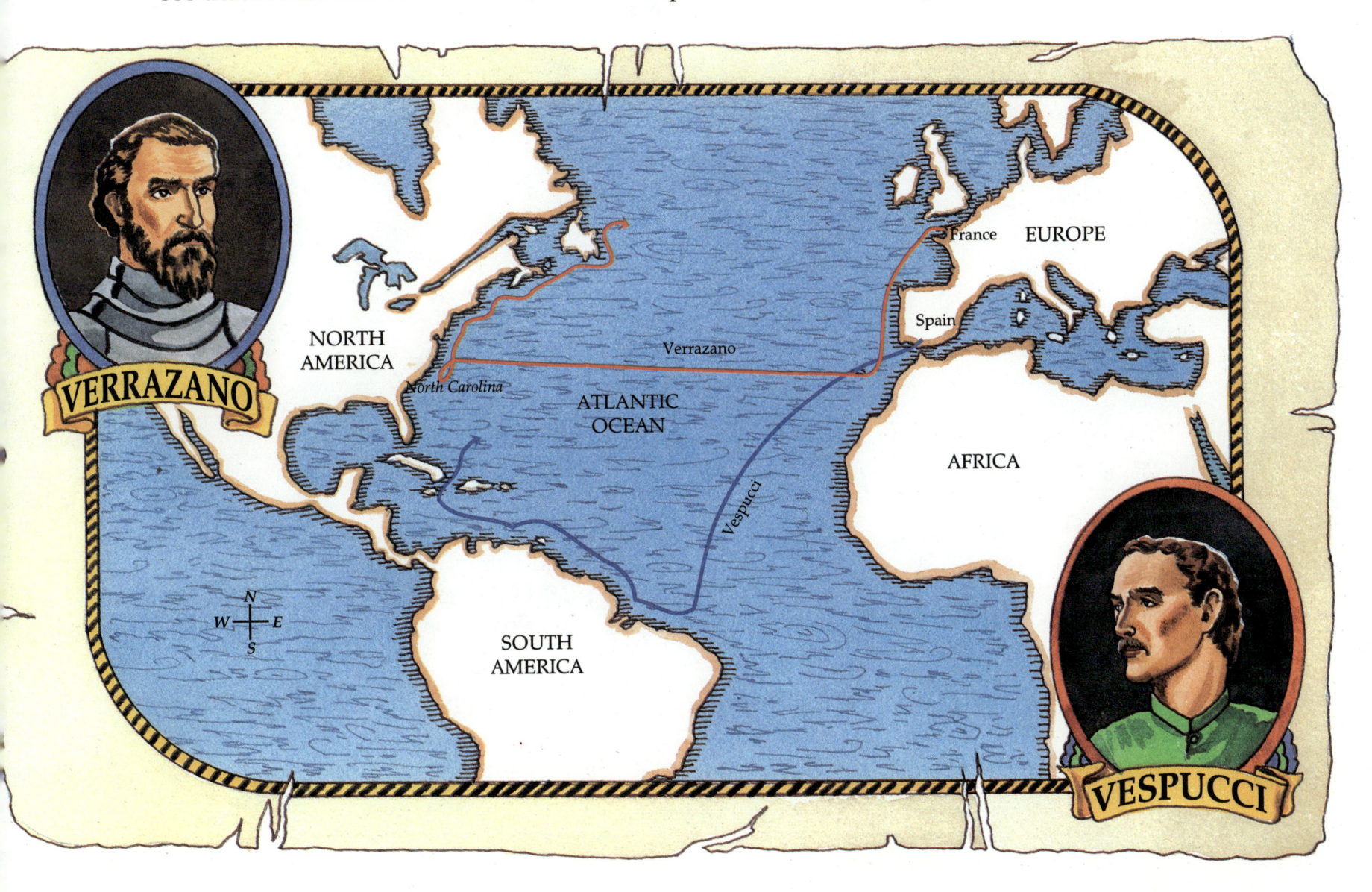

The Conquistador

Rumors had long told of vast riches and mighty empires hidden in the mysterious heartland of what is now South America. Balboa had gone in search of the wealth of the Incas and had found the Pacific Ocean instead. In 1518 a Spanish conquistador (or "conqueror") named Hernán Cortés was chosen by the governor of Cuba to find out once and for all if the stories were true.

He nearly failed before he even set out. In 1518 a group of his enemies convinced the governor that Cortés was a traitor. Orders went out to arrest him. But Cortés would not be stopped. He avoided capture by moving from place to place and, in February 1519, led a fleet of eleven ships and six hundred men to sea.

EMPIRE OF THE AZTECS

He landed on the Gulf coast of Mexico. The people who lived there, called Tabascans, had never seen ships, guns, or horses. They believed the white-skinned Spaniards to be gods. A young woman who could speak the languages of inland Mexico became Cortés's interpreter. The Spaniards called her Lady Marina.

Through her, Cortés learned of a great empire that ruled the high mountains inland. A warlike people, the Aztecs had built their empire by conquest. They were then trying to conquer the Tlascalans, who were fighting back fiercely.

Cortés founded a town he named Veracruz and spent the next few months learning as much as he could about the Aztecs. He also did a remarkable thing: He burned all of his ships so that no man could turn back.

Meanwhile, the Aztecs were also learning about the Spaniards. Montezuma, the Aztec emperor, listened to the amazing news of the white-skinned strangers. They worried him. Who knew what powers they had? They might even be gods, for Aztec legends told of white-skinned gods who would come to Earth someday.

Half in awe, half in fear, Montezuma sent the strangers gifts of gold and silver. It was to prove a terrible mistake. The rich gifts told Cortés exactly what he had hoped: He had found the empire of gold that Spain had been seeking for so long.

Gods on Horseback

In August, Cortés led 415 soldiers and horsemen inland to the Aztec capital of Tenochtitlán. With the interpreter's help, he carefully made friends with many of the tribes along the way. At one point the fierce Tlascalans barred his way. But Cortés brought these warriors into a partnership against the Aztecs. The Tlascalans may have cooperated with Cortés because they were amazed by the Spanish cavalry. Like other native Americans, they had never seen a "horse-man."

After weeks of hard climbing, Cortés's army and native allies finally reached the heights above Tenochtitlán. There they saw a wondrous sight. A gleaming city, larger than any in Spain, lay before them, set in the middle of a vast lake. Causeways linked the many islands. Great temples honored the Aztec gods, and broad avenues were filled with brightly dressed people.

CAPTURING THE EMPEROR

Still uncertain, afraid to insult these strangers who might be gods, Montezuma welcomed them into his city. The Spaniards were given one of the grandest palaces to live in, and they soon began to talk with the Aztecs about trade. But Cortés heard rumors that Montezuma was planning an attack; perhaps the emperor had finally decided that the Spaniards were men rather than gods.

Cortés moved fast. Marching to the emperor's palace, his men took Montezuma prisoner. With the emperor in chains, Cortés felt that his conquest was complete, for the Aztecs would not attack if it would bring harm to Montezuma.

But Cortés had no time to enjoy his victory. Word soon reached him that the governor of Cuba, who still hoped to arrest him, had sent armed men to Veracruz. Cortés hurried back with a small force and defeated the governor's soldiers. He threw some into prison, while the rest agreed to join his army. In June 1520, Cortés returned to Tenochtitlán, where more trouble awaited him.

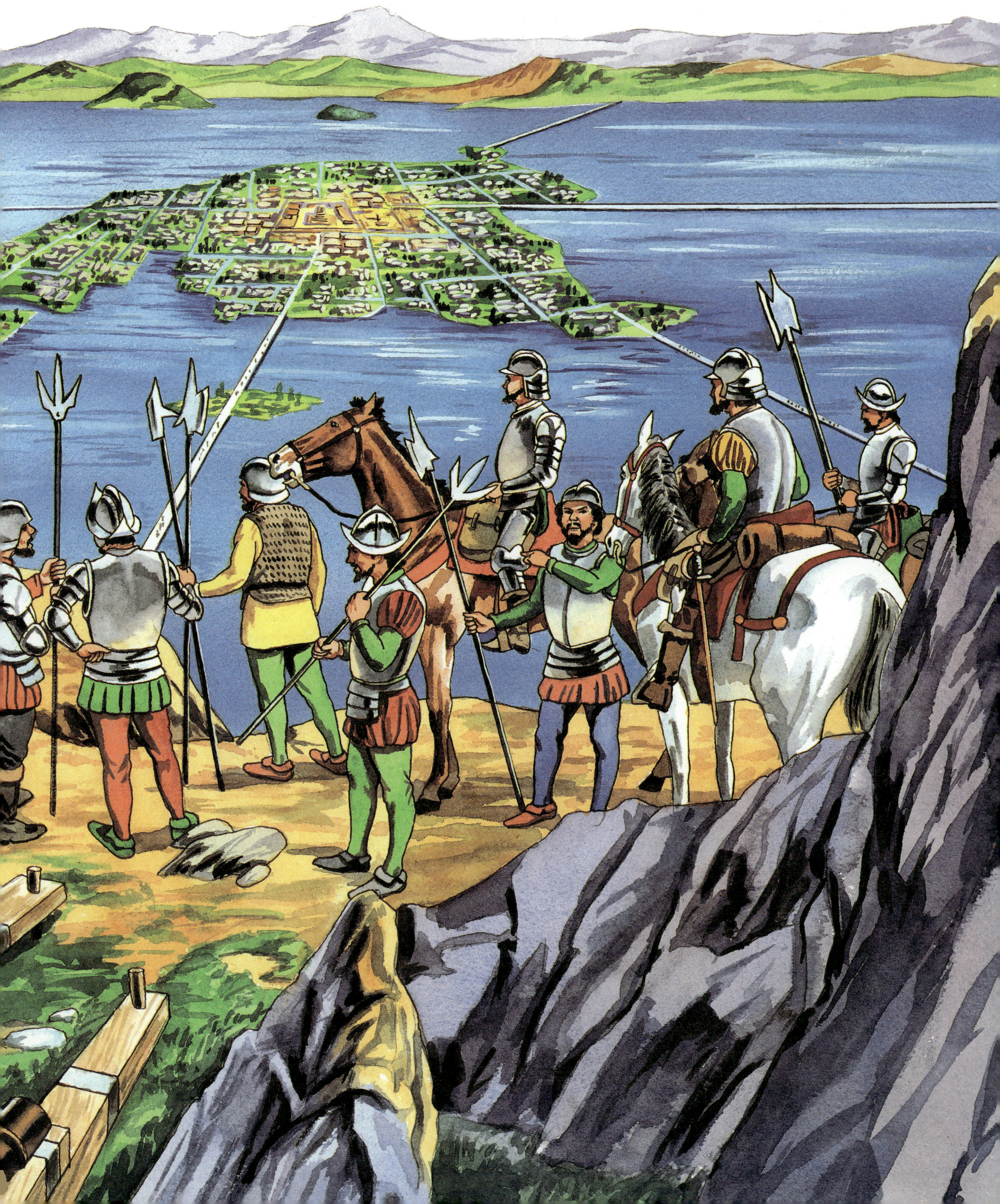

The Sad Night

While Cortés was away, his men did something they would regret. Horrified by the Aztec religion, which included bloody sacrifices, they broke up a religious festival. They drove off the Aztecs and turned the temple into a Christian church. Perhaps they hoped to make Christians of the Aztecs. They may have thought that without the emperor the Aztecs would accept this change. The Spaniards were wrong.

Cortés returned to find his men prisoners, surrounded by a large Aztec army. After Cortés learned what had happened, he decided to send Montezuma out to speak with the Aztec people. It did no good—the people refused to listen. The enraged Aztecs hurled stones and knocked the emperor to the ground. Montezuma died three days later, and Cortés knew that he and his men must fight their way out or be killed.

The Spanish called it *la noche triste*, "the sad night." As the armed and armored Spaniards marched from the palace, the vengeful Aztecs fell upon them. Cortés and his men pressed desperately onward, their keen swords flashing. In the long night's battle, they lost their gold treasure, their guns, their horses, and—many of them—their lives. Only about one hundred, including Cortés and the lady interpreter, made it back to the land of their Tlascalan allies.

FINAL VICTORY

Less than a year later, in May 1521, Cortés returned to Tenochtitlán, this time at the head of a full army. By August he had ruthlessly destroyed the city. The Spanish were now free to enslave the Aztecs who still lived and to strip the empire of its wealth.

Cortés's victory over the Aztecs made him governor of all Mexico. But he did not wear his title in peace. The Spanish began fighting among themselves for money and power, and Cortés was in the thick of it. He sailed backed to Spain in 1528 and again in 1540 to win the king's favor after enemies had brought charges against him. In 1547 he was about to return to Mexico when he died, at the age of sixty-two. The conquistador asked that his body be sent to the Mexico he had conquered with gunpowder and steel.

The Keeper of Pigs

With the conquest of the Aztecs, gold and silver began to flow from the New World to Spain. And Aztec gold was only the beginning. For another Spanish conquistador was soon to claim the riches of the greatest empire in the Americas.

Francisco Pizarro spent his early life as a keeper of pigs in Spain. Poverty drove him to soldiering and then, in his mid-twenties, to the New World. He scratched out a living there as a fighting man. Pizarro's luck began to turn in 1513, when he joined Balboa's expedition in search of the land of the Incas. With Balboa, he saw the Pacific Ocean glittering in the afternoon sun.

THE DISCOVERY OF PERU

Pizarro settled in Panama and was given enough land to lead a comfortable life. But dreams of conquest stayed with him. In 1524, and again in 1526, Pizarro led expeditions south. On the second voyage, he discovered the coast of Peru and was welcomed by a rich Inca. He brought enough gold back to prove that the legends of the Incas were true. But the governor of Panama refused to allow another expedition.

Pizarro decided to go to Spain to see the king. His partners—one of whom was another soldier named Diego de Almagro—agreed. In 1529 the king gave permission for the expedition. He named Pizarro governor of any new lands he conquered. When Pizarro returned to Panama, Almagro became bitterly jealous of the greater honors given to Pizarro by the king. And thus Pizzaro acquired an enemy he could not afford to have.

NORTH AMERICA
ATLANTIC OCEAN
Panama
SOUTH AMERICA
Peru
PACIFIC OCEAN
N
W
E
S

The Fall of the Incas

In January 1531 Pizarro sailed south from Panama with three ships, about one hundred and eighty men, horses, and two small cannons. Almagro remained behind to raise more money and gather more men.

Pizarro was now nearly sixty, a determined, ruthless man. Landing in Peru, he climbed into the Andes Mountains, where the Inca Empire covered some two thousand miles. The Incas built great highways and beautiful bridges, but no carriages traveled these roads, for the Incas had never invented the wheel.

Like the Aztecs, the Incas believed in a myth about white gods, and the Spaniards filled them with doubt and confusion. And as they would soon learn, their weapons were no match for Spanish swords and guns.

TREACHERY AND WEALTH

The young Inca emperor, Atahualpa, chose not to attack, and Pizarro took over the city of Cajamarca. With his men hidden nearby, Pizarro invited the emperor and his men into the city square for a talk. Once the Incas were inside the square, Spanish cannons roared and the terrible soldiers on horseback charged. Incas died by the thousands. The emperor became Pizarro's prisoner.

Pizarro promised Atahualpa his freedom if the Incas would fill his prison cell with treasure. The Incas brought the Spanish invaders thirteen thousand two hundred and sixty-five pounds of gold and twenty-six thousand pounds of silver: more than $90 million at today's prices. When this wealth was safely in his hands, Pizarro had the young emperor tied to a stake and murdered.

Tragically, this treachery served Pizarro well. The Inca army fell apart. For the next four years, Pizarro and Almagro expanded their rule over the entire empire. Pizarro even convinced Almagro to try to conquer the neighboring land of Chile. The attack failed, and in bitterness and jealousy, Almagro turned on his partner. The two men led armies against each other, until, in 1538, Pizarro's men captured and killed Almagro.

But Almagro took revenge from his grave. A band of his men killed Francisco Pizarro in his palace on June 26, 1541. The conquistador, who had lived by treachery and the sword, finally died by the weapons that had won him so much.

Heroes and Rogues

Some explorers sailed for riches and glory. Others really wanted to know what lay beyond the distant horizon. Explorers all, these heroes and rogues of the sixteenth century set a pattern that many would follow.

Francis Drake, an Englishman, was the first. Half explorer, half pirate, he was raiding Spanish treasure ships in 1579 when he reached the southern tip of South America. He sailed on into the Pacific Ocean and raided Spanish outposts. Soon his ship was full of treasure, but the Spaniards were searching for him now. Which way could he go without falling into their hands?

He sailed north and explored the coast of California, hoping to find a way around North America. But he found none. He then decided to risk sailing across the Pacific for England, which he finally reached in 1580, the second captain to circle the world.

The explorations of Drake and others gave England a claim to North America. But France and Holland sent their own explorers. In fact, it was Henry Hudson, sailing for Holland, and Samuel de Champlain, a French nobleman, who made the most important discoveries. They found no gold but riches of another sort: farmland and forests, oceans and rivers teeming with fish, and streams full of beaver. It was a land where people could make a home. It eventually became the homeland of Europeans and others who claimed it as their own.

Today's explorers are scientists who plot their courses with computers. But they should never forget their ancestry: those heroes and rogues of old who fought shamelessly for their own glory and that of their kings. That passion will always be part of the explorer's spirit.

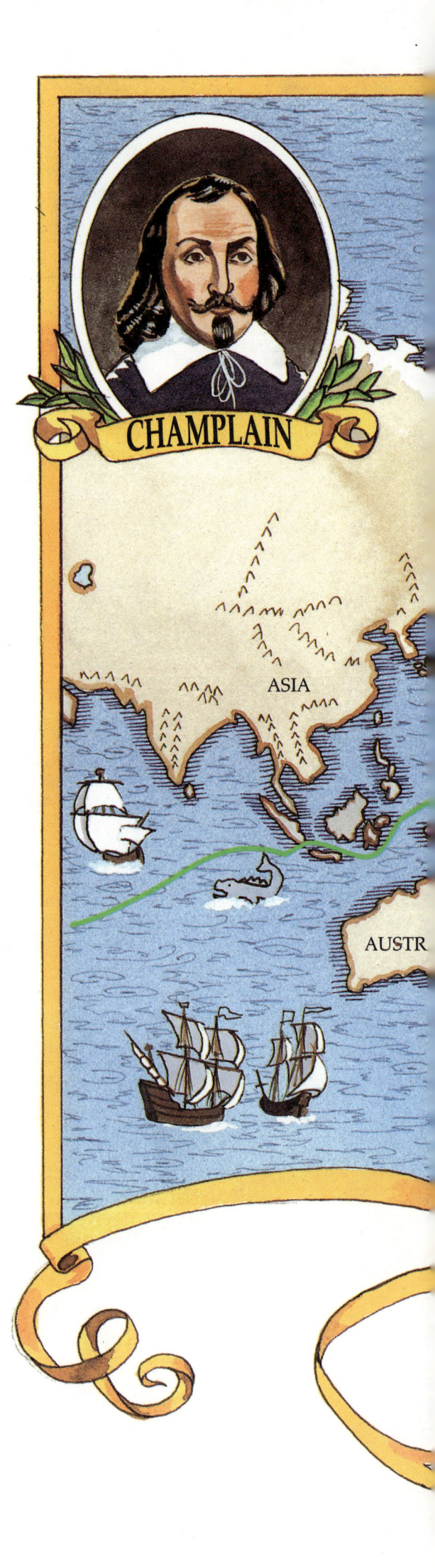

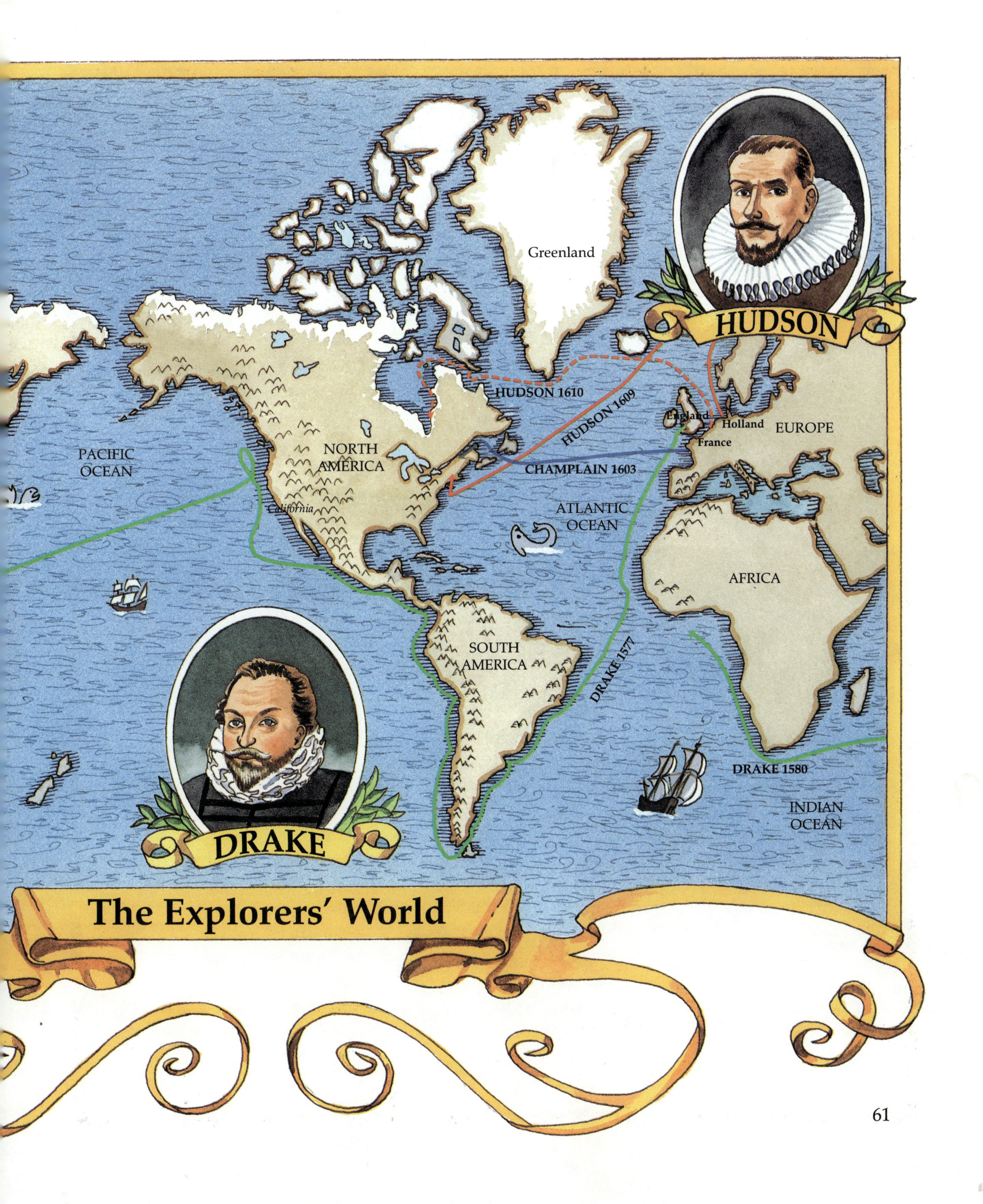

The Explorers' World

Index

Africa, 40, 41, 48
Almagro, Diego de, 56, 58, 59
America, naming of, 49
Arawaks, 28-29, 32, 33
Astrolabe, 25
Atahualpa, 58-59
Aztecs, 51-56, 58
Bahamas, 26
Balboa, Vasco Núñez de, 38-39, 50, 56
Brazil, 40
Calicut, 42, 43
Cape of Good Hope, 14, 16, 41, 42
Caribbean Sea, 32
Cathay, 10, 11, 30
Champlain, Samuel de, 60
China, 10
Cipangu, 29, 30
Columbus, Christopher, 6-37
   as child, 8
   at Cuba, 29, 30, 32
   at Hispaniola, 30, 32, 33, 35
   at Jamaica, 32, 36
   at San Salvador, 26-29
   death of, 36
   discovery of South America, 34
   dream of reaching Asia by going west, 14, 16, 19, 36
   first expedition, 23-30
   fourth expedition, "High Voyage," 36
   in chains, 35
   in Lisbon, 11
   in sea battle, 11
   in the Caribbean, 32
   journal, 23
   logbooks, 23

Columbus (continued)
   marooned, 36
   return to Spain, 31, 33-34, 35, 36
   sailing experience, 8, 11
   second expedition, 32
   sighting of land, 25
   support for mission of, 16-21
   third expedition, 34-35
Columbus, Diego, 32
Cortés, Hernán, 50-55
Cuba, 29, 30, 32, 52
Da Gama, Vasco, 41-43
Dias, Bartholomeu, 14, 19, 41, 42
Dominican Republic, 30
Drake, Francis, 60
England, 60
Ferdinand, King, 20-21, 26, 31, 32, 33, 34, 35, 36
Gagarin, Yuri, 7
Guam, 47
Haiti, 30
Hispaniola, 30, 32, 33, 35, 36, 38
Holland, 60
Hudson, Henry, 60
Iceland, 13-14
Incas, 39, 56, 58-59
India, 40, 42, 44
Indian Ocean, 41, 48
Indians, 7
International Date Line, 48
Isabella (colony), 32
Isabella, Queen, 20-21, 26, 31, 32, 33, 34, 35, 36
Jamaica, 32, 36
Japan, 29
John II, King, 14, 16
Knots as measure, 25

Kublai Khan, 10
Magellan, Ferdinand, 44-48
Manuel, King, 43
Moluccas, 44, 46
Montezuma, 51, 52, 54
Mozambique, 42
Navidad, 30, 32
Newfoundland, 13
Niña, 21
Pacific Ocean, 36, 39, 47, 60
Peru, 56, 58
Panama, 36, 38, 39, 56, 58
Pedrarias, 39
Philippines, 47
Pinta, 21, 25
Pizarro, Francisco, 56-59
Polo, Marco, 9, 10
Portugal, 11 14, 16, 19, 40-43, 44, 46, 49
Rustichello, 10
San Salvador, 26, 28-29
Santa María, 21, 23
Santangel, Luis de, 20
Sea monsters, 9
South America, 34, 49, 50
Spain, 7, 20-21, 31, 35, 36, 38, 39, 40, 46, 49
Spice Islands, 44, 46
Strait of Magellan, 46-47
Tabascans, 51
Tenochtitlán, 52, 54, 55
Tlascalans, 51, 52
Tobacco, 30
Trinidad, 48
Veracruz, 51, 52
Verrazano, Giovanni da, 49
Vespucci, Amerigo, 49
Victoria, 48

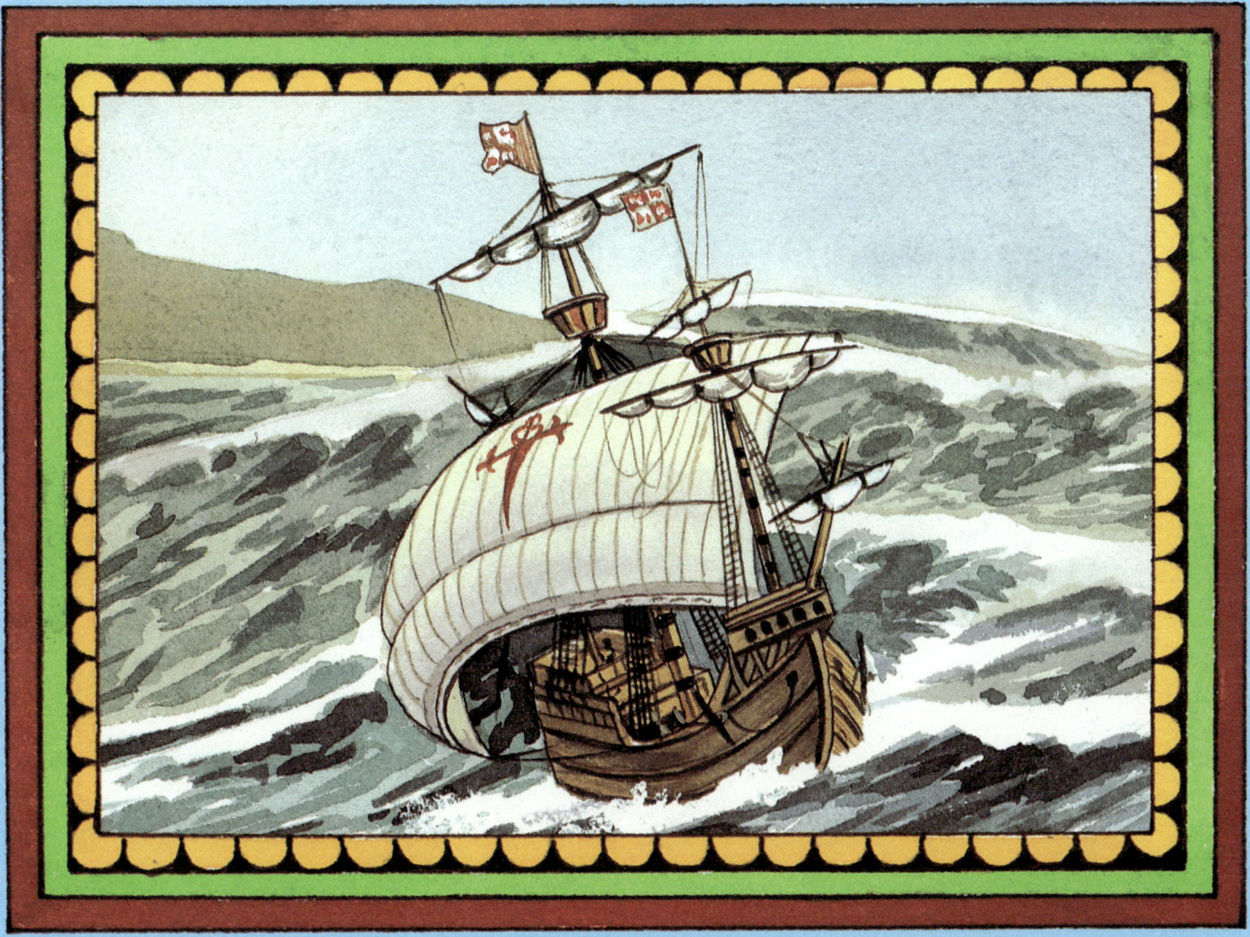